FOR PARENTS OF PRESCHOOLERS
AGES 0-5

RAISING GREAT KIDS

**PARTICIPANT'S
GUIDE**

Resources by Henry Cloud and John Townsend

Boundaries
Boundaries Workbook
Boundaries audio
Boundaries curriculum
Boundaries in Dating
Boundaries in Dating Workbook
Boundaries in Dating audio
Boundaries in Dating curriculum
Boundaries in Marriage
Boundaries in Marriage Workbook
Boundaries in Marriage audio
Boundaries in Marriage curriculum
Boundaries with Kids
Boundaries with Kids Workbook
Boundaries with Kids audio
Boundaries with Kids curriculum
Changes That Heal (Cloud)
Changes That Heal Workbook (Cloud)
Changes That Heal audio (Cloud)
Hiding from Love (Townsend)
How People Grow
How People Grow Workbook
How People Grow audio
How to Have That Difficult Conversation You've Been Avoiding
Making Small Groups Work
Making Small Groups Work audio
The Mom Factor
The Mom Factor Workbook
Raising Great Kids
Raising Great Kids audio
Raising Great Kids for Parents of Preschoolers curriculum
Raising Great Kids Workbook for Parents of Preschoolers
Raising Great Kids Workbook for Parents of School-Age Children
Raising Great Kids Workbook for Parents of Teenagers
Safe People
Safe People Workbook
12 "Christian" Beliefs That Can Drive You Crazy

FOR PARENTS OF PRESCHOOLERS

AGES 0-5

Dr. Henry Cloud & Dr. John Townsend

WITH LISA GUEST

RAISING GREAT KIDS

PARTICIPANT'S
GUIDE

A COMPREHENSIVE GUIDE TO
Parenting with Grace and Truth

ZONDERVAN®

GRAND RAPIDS, MICHIGAN 49530 USA

MOTHERS OF
MOPS.
PRESCHOOLERS
...because mothering matters

ZONDERVAN.COM/
AUTHORTRACKER

ZONDERVAN®

Raising Great Kids for Parents of Preschoolers Participant's Guide
Copyright © 2000 by Henry Cloud and John Townsend

Requests for information should be addressed to:

Zondervan, *Grand Rapids, Michigan 49530*

ISBN-10: 0-310-23295-3
ISBN-13: 978-0-310-23295-7

Published in association with Yates & Greer, LLP, Literary Agent, Orange, CA.

Interior design by Laura Klynstra Blost

Printed in the United States of America

07 08 09 10 11 12 • 16 15 14 13 12 11 10 9 8

—Contents—

—Foreword—

At MOPS International—an organization that encourages and supports mothers of young children—we are often asked what resource we recommend on the elusive and challenging subject of parenting.

Well, here it is!

With all the fantastic curriculums available today, how can we choose *Raising Great Kids for Parents of Preschoolers* as our favorite? Three reasons:

First, it works. It speaks the language moms and dads speak. It makes sense. We can *get* this stuff. When I consider the everydayness of parenting, Drs. Henry Cloud and John Townsend provide principles and techniques that work.

Second, it's biblical. With both theological and psychological training to their credit, the authors offer us an integrated and trustworthy perspective. They've done their homework and offer us the results.

Third, it's foundational. This curriculum underlines the unique importance of the early years. As parents, it's great to begin with the end in mind. I can see the results of this parenting approach played out in the character of my own kids. No, they're not perfect. But they are great!

So, as the president of MOPS International and as the mother of two growing and going children, I believe this curriculum is the best resource for guiding us through the parenting process with preschoolers. If you're just beginning your parenting journey, like many moms and dads of preschoolers, there is help for you here.

ELISA MORGAN
PRESIDENT AND CEO,
MOTHERS OF PRESCHOOLERS (MOPS), INC.

—Preface—

Raising kids of character is a daunting task, so there's no better time to start than when they're young!

The first few years of life is the most critical period of growth and development. Infants start the process of trusting the love of Mom and Dad and God, toddlers begin experiencing freedom and responsibility, and children start understanding how to function in the real world. In short, this is the period in which a child's soul is developed.

As a parent, you are right at the center of that process. It's impossible to overestimate how important a role you play in rearing your child. As the Bible teaches, God shows us how to trust in him "even at my mother's breast" (Psalm 22:9). But most parents feel overwhelmed by the complexity of the job. With so many things to worry about, how do you know the real tasks and goals of parenting? Many moms and dads become discouraged or don't know where to start. We wrote *Raising Great Kids* and developed this curriculum to help you.

In this video curriculum—just as in the book—we offer you a structure for approaching parenting. We provide a road map for creating *character* in your children—the ability to function as God designed them to function in the world. The biblical principles set forth in the book apply to all ages and stages of kids, so you can use them as a guide for all the years you parent. This video curriculum, however, deals specifically with infants, toddlers, and preschoolers. It addresses, in a practical, hands-on manner, situations and issues you encounter with children five years old and younger. Our goal is to help empower parents of these children—moms and dads like you—to become intentional and effective in your parenting.

We're glad you've decided to invest the time and effort in your children by working through *Raising Great Kids for Parents of Preschoolers*.

We pray that God will use this study to help your parenting be the successful and worthwhile relationship he designed it to be. We appreciate your labors as a parent—and may God bless you!

HENRY CLOUD, PH.D.
JOHN TOWNSEND, PH.D.

—Session One—
Raising Children of Character

OVERVIEW

✢ The parent's task is to develop a little person into an adult. The issue along the way is not simply about the child's being good, but about having good character.

✢ Character is *the sum of our abilities to deal with life as God designed us to.*

✢ As a child grows up, parents transfer more and more freedom and responsibility from their shoulders to their child's.

✢ Growing character in children always involves the elements of development and internalizing.

FOUR FUNDAMENTAL FACTORS IN EFFECTIVE PARENTING

- We provide a road map for creating *character* in our children—the ability to function as God designed them to function in the world.
- There are four fundamental factors in effective parenting:

  - *The value of love.* Relationship is central to parenting. To develop, your child is going to need to be deeply related to you and others, and you are going to have to keep relationship as a goal of her development.
  - *The value of truth.* Children cannot be loved too much, but they can be disciplined too little. As a parent, you are a dispenser of truth and reality. The goal is to have your child become a person of truth, living in wisdom.
  - *The value of freedom.* You must require responsibility from your children. Then you'll be helping them grow into free people who have learned how to use their freedom to choose good things—things like love, responsibility, service, and accomplishment.
  - *The role of God.* Character is never complete without an understanding of who one is before God. God gave parents the assignment of bringing up children to understand him and to take their proper place before him.

- Because children have free will, there is no guarantee that children will turn out right. You are responsible for the process, but God is in charge of the results. This series is designed to help you with the process.
- God's plan for parenting is outlined in the Bible. If you violate any of God's principles, both you and your child will pay.
- Pray hard, get lots of support, implement suggestions you'll find in *Raising Great Kids*, and enjoy your kids.

"Who Is Responsible for What?"

- Who is responsible for our child's maturity and readiness for the world—us or our children?
- Responsibility lies on a _____ between child and parent, and its position on the continuum _____ over time. As a child grows up, parents _____ more and more freedom and responsibility from their shoulders to their child's.
- Even though responsibility shifts, both parents and children still have their own unique and distinct _____. Parents provide _____ and _____, and they also structure experiences to help the child mature. The child responds to these experiences, takes _____, _____, and learns _____. Parents and children can't do each other's jobs; they must each do their own.
- _____ must bear the ultimate _____ for their lives. Children always need to be moving toward full responsibility for their lives and souls.

ENCOURAGING RESPONSIBILITY

Directions

The three questions listed below are designed to help you start now to teach your children how to take responsibility for their lives. Turn to two or three people near you (ideally not your spouse so that you'll have more ideas to share afterwards) and spend the next 10 minutes answering these questions. If you have time, there is a fourth question for you to discuss.

1. Children must bear the ultimate responsibility for their lives. What experiences can you structure to help your preschooler take on greater responsibility? For example, what kind of schedule and system of rules for doing chores—and what consequences for not doing them—could you establish?

2. The child's tasks are to take risks, fail, and learn lessons. What risks have you seen your young one take? How have you responded— or how do you want to respond—to your child's risk-taking and failures?

3. To both keep good limits and stay emotionally connected with your child when she disobeys, what will you do and say? Imagine, for instance, that your heartbroken child has temporarily lost a much-loved toy to time out because he or she misused it.

If Time Allows

4. What, if anything, did you learn before first grade about the fact that you are ultimately responsible for your life?

THE ASPECTS OF CHARACTER

- **Connectedness**—the most basic and important character ability—is the ability to form relationships. Children need to learn to need, trust, depend, and have empathy for others. When your child falls down and skins her knee, your comfort helps her to experience and learn the value of reaching out.
- **Responsibility** is the second important aspect of character. Your child is born thinking her life is *your* problem. But part of growing character is helping her to take ownership over her life and to see her life as her problem.
- **Reality** is the ability to accept the negatives of the real world. You need to help her deal with sin, loss, failure, and evil, not only in herself, but in others and in the world.
- **Competence** is key to character. Children need training to develop their God-given gifts and talents. They need to develop their skill not only in specialty areas such as art, sports, or science, but also in everyday matters, such as decision making, judgment, and work ethics.
- **Morality** is an internal sense of right and wrong. The development of a conscience is a process.
- **Worship** is essential to being a person of character. Created in the image of God, children need to learn that God loves them and is in charge of life. They also need to learn to seek God on their own, apart from their parents.
- These character aspects are attributes of God's own character. The difference is that while God has always had these character traits, your child is in the process of developing them. So your first, last, and best goal is to be a good agent of developing mature character within your child's life and soul.
- Growing your child's character always involves two elements: development, or training through experience and practice; and internalizing, or taking those experiences inside to become a part of his personality.

MAKING IT HAPPEN

GROWING CHARACTER IN YOUR CHILD

Directions

For our last exercise, spend 8 minutes on your own thinking about the two questions below. The goal of this time is to come up with one thing you can do now to help your child develop each of the six aspects of character.

1. Each of us can learn from the parenting we received. We can learn both how do to certain things well and what we want to avoid doing now that we are parents. What did your parents do right (or wrong) to help you develop each of the following character traits?

   Connectedness—the ability to form relationships

   Responsibility—taking ownership of their own life and seeing their life as their problem

   Reality—the ability to accept the negatives of the real world

   Competence—the development of everyday life skills as well as their God-given gifts and talents

   Morality—an internal sense of right and wrong

   Worship—learning that God loves them and is in charge of life; learning to seek God on their own

2. What is one thing you can do now to help your child develop each of the following aspects of character?

Connectedness

Responsibility

Reality

Competence

Morality

Worship

Suggested Reading

For more on this session's material, read "The Goal of Parenting: A Child with Character," the first chapter in *Raising Great Kids*.

Taking It Home

- Look again at the list of ideas you wrote down in the exercise "Growing Character in Your Child." Choose one or two of these ideas to implement this week.
- Try to become more aware of what you're modeling about each of the six aspects of character.
- This week and every week—during this course and afterwards—pray for your kids: Ask the Lord to soften their hearts so that the Spirit can help them develop into people of godly character. And pray for your parenting: Ask God to help you seize opportunities to help your kids develop the traits of connectedness, responsibility, reality, competence, morality, and worship.

—*Session Two*—
Ingredients for Growth: Grace, Truth, and Time

OVERVIEW

- ✢ Parents need to show children grace, to show that they are on their children's side.
- ✢ Parents need to give children truth, to give them reality and necessary limits.
- ✢ Grace helps children tolerate dealing with truth.
- ✢ Along with grace and truth, time is the third necessary element of growth.
- ✢ Time allows the process of character growth in children to occur continuously.
- ✢ Grace + Truth over Time = Growth

VIDEO SEGMENT

GRACE AND TRUTH DIVIDED

- The problem parents face is that the very ingredients needed for growth—grace and truth—are divided against one another. Choosing between the two is not the problem. Getting them together is. An effective parent must learn to be gracious and truthful at the same time.
- *Grace* means "favor," and usually this favor is spoken of as "unmerited." In other words, true grace is not earned: it is given freely out of love.
- Grace shows itself in kindness, empathy, forgiveness, compassion, understanding, provision, love, and help.
- *Truth* is the state of being reliable and trustworthy. It is ultimately reality, the timeless realities God wove into his creation. If we live in truth, we do what is right. In addition, a truthful person is someone who faces what "really is."
- Truth shows itself in morality, standards, expectations, evaluations, judgment, confrontation, discipline, limits, honesty, and integrity.
- Both grace and truth are important, but getting them together is difficult. It's too easy to give love without limits or limits without love. An effective parent must learn to be gracious and truthful at the same time.
- Children need to know that parents are on their side. As grace is taught and modeled, as parents let their child know that "we are for you," grace is experienced and internalized by the child.
- Grace and truth need to come together in parenting. For example, during a child's temper tantrum, the parent needs to stay emotionally connected to the child even though he is behaving badly. At the same time, the parent needs to hold to the truth, to the standard that the behavior is, in fact, unacceptable. By doing so, grace and truth come together for the child.

BRINGING GRACE AND TRUTH TOGETHER

Directions

1. Split into groups of 3.
2. Keeping in mind the discussion about the integration of grace and truth, talk together about how you can help your children see that reality, or truth, is *for* them, not *against* them. For example, you might teach your child that if he shows restraint and doesn't whine to have cookies at the store, he avoids losing the toy he brought along in the car during the ride home.* Choose two or three real-life situations and talk about how you can integrate grace and truth, how you can be soft on the person but hard on the issue.
3. You will have 8 minutes for this exercise.

Situations

1.

2.

3.

---

*If your child is still an infant, conflicts aren't yet an issue. So consider a hypothetical situation like a toddler throwing a toy after the parent has said not to, or a preschooler refusing to get dressed when asked.

- For each situation you listed, note what the child might be feeling (tired, frustrated, angry, etc.). With what words could you speak to such feelings? What actions would communicate empathy and grace?

- What limits do you need to set in each situation? With what words could you clearly set and stick by those limits? What actions would also express that truth?

Video Segment

The Ingredient of Time

- "Quality time" versus "quantity time" is a false choice society often presents parents. Quantity of time is important because growth is happening—continuously—and you must be there throughout the process.
- Quantity of time is also important because children internalize things from the outside world as they grow, so parents have to be constantly monitoring what their children internalize. Like a car's gas tank, you need to distribute the fuel as the child needs it.
- Quantity of time is important because children need to grow in relationship with another person in order to develop character.
- Internalizing a new skill, habit, or moral teaching is a process—one that involves ignorance, failure, and disobedience on the part of the child, and discipline, encouragement, and teaching on the part of the parent. And the five steps of the process of teaching and internalizing character require time.

   Step 1. Introduce children to the reality.
   Step 2. Allow children to experience the limits of their abilities.
   Step 3. Transform the failure.
   Step 4. Help the child to identify with the reality.
   Step 5. Encourage your child to try again.

- Time must be integrated with the other two important ingredients we've already addressed—grace and truth. Grace + Truth over Time = Growth

MAKING TIME, BUILDING SKILLS

1. Quantity of time is important to the development of children of character. How much time in a typical day and week are you intentionally investing in your children? "Intentionally investing" means focusing on the child's growth, not simply watching TV together or running errands with him tagging along. It might mean, for instance, time spent playing, reading, or teaching a skill.

2. What does your answer to the preceding question suggest about your parenting?

3. Children cannot accomplish certain tasks before they're developmentally (neurologically, physically) ready. In what area of life or toward what behavioral goal might you be pushing your toddler or preschooler too much?

4. In what areas of life, if any, could you be encouraging your child to move ahead? Be specific about your plan—and ask someone to hold you accountable to this resolution.

Suggested Reading

"The Ingredients of Grace and Truth" and "The Ingredient of Time," chapters 2 and 3 of *Raising Great Kids*

Taking It Home

1. In one of the session's videos, Dr. Cloud said, "Character development requires experience. You can't tell children how to do something and expect them to do it correctly. Instead, you must walk them through the process, help them when they fail, and aid them in making normal failure a learning experience that becomes part of their character. We feel strongly that time is a necessary ingredient for growth."

   What did you learn about failure as you were growing up?

   What might you do to help your child make normal failure a learning experience?

2. Review the five steps of teaching and internalizing character listed below:

- *Introduce children to the reality*—a concept, rule, or behavior. Don't expect your children to know what you expect.
- *Allow children to experience the limits of their abilities.* Kids will hit the reality limit—fail at a new skill or choose to disobey a new rule. If inherent rebellion is behind the failure, the parent must set a limit by saying that to disobey a rule is "not okay." When the failure is not due to rebellion, parents should offer correction and encouragement, not punishment.
- *Transform the failure.* When failure and discipline hurt, empathize with and contain your child's feelings. Empathy paves the way for children to identify with the limit or reality of their performance. In contrast, anger, guilt, and shame distance them from the reality they need to internalize.
- *Help the child identify with the reality.* If children feel understood and loved while they see the reality of their actions (#3), they will take in the reality of the rule. It becomes part of them.
- *Encourage your child to try again*—to develop the new skill, the obey the new rule, or to adapt the behavior. When learning, children have to try and fail and then try again.

Now, apply the above process to two current parenting issues with your toddler or preschooler (issues such as not hitting, staying at the table during a meal, saying "please," or putting toys away).

Situation #1	Situation #2
1.	1.
2.	2.
3.	3.
4.	4.
5.	5.

3. What plan will you make for regularly spending time with your child? Of course, what you do together will change as your child grows, but it's not too early to start enjoying one-on-one time with your child. So when will you go out for ice cream or visit the local park? Establishing a schedule (ex. every other Saturday) is a good starting point for investing time in your child and fueling her tank with love and limits.

4. Remember to pray for your kids this week!

—Session Three—

Developing Connectedness and Responsibility

OVERVIEW

✣ *Connectedness* is the capacity to relate to God and others on a deeply personal level. It is foundational to all growth and morality.

✣ The development of connectedness in children requires specific tasks on the part of both parent and child.

✣ *Responsibility* is the capacity to own one's life as one's problem.

✣ Self-control and learning limits are necessary for responsibly choosing the good and refusing the bad.

✣ The four qualities involved in teaching kids responsibility are love, truth, freedom, and reality.

LAYING THE FOUNDATION OF LIFE: CONNECTEDNESS

- Connectedness is the capacity to relate to God and others. When we make an attachment, good things—such as empathy, comfort, truth, and encouragement—are transferred between us and others. Connectedness brings warmth, meaning, and purpose to life.

- The ability to connect is a character trait. When a person is loved and treated well, she attaches to the person who loves her and treats her well. She gains a sense that being loved and treated well is a good thing. In addition, she learns how to love and treat others well. This is the basis of the Golden Rule, the foundation of all morality. All of the tasks of life are based, at some level, on how attached we are to God and others.

- Life brings many demands, problems, and requirements. Connected children look within themselves for what they can provide, and then go to God and others for the rest. Detached children fend for themselves, unable to reach out for resources and help. Dylan and Spencer were very different kids and therefore took very different approaches to a similar problem. Dylan knew he couldn't deal with the problem himself, so he went to his mom and received comfort, support, and structure so that together they could solve the problem. His brother, Spencer, had not reached out to include family and friends when confronted with a problem.

- The child who is allowed to emotionally depend on a reliable, loving parent becomes fortified with the assurance of her stability. As a child internalizes her mother's love, she feels safe enough to explore the world confidently.

- The first year of life is critical to the development of attachment capacities in a child. After that, start working on some specific attachment goals for your child: using relationship for equilibrium, learning basic trust and need, valuing relationships, internalizing love, developing a capacity for loss, developing gender roles, relating to the world, developing give-and-take, and being altruistic.

- Connectedness truly is foundational to all morality and stands as the most important trait we'll look at.

MAKING IT HAPPEN

CONNECTING TO YOUR YOUNG CHILD

1. What are you doing to establish attachment with your child early in his or her life?

2. What words or actions most clearly communicate love to your child? If you're not sure, become a student of your child: which of your words and actions seem to most effectively make your child feel loved?

NINE ATTACHMENT GOALS: WHAT'S A PARENT TO DO?

Directions

1. Divide the large group into nine groups of two or three people.
2. Each group will be assigned one goal to discuss. (If time allows and numbers necessitate, an alternative plan would be to assign two goals to a group.)
3. When we come back together as a large group, a spokesperson from each group will share with the rest of us that group's ideas about how to help kids attach in that particular way.
4. You'll have eight minutes to complete this exercise.

Goal #1: Use relationship for equilibrium. Good attachment stabilizes children. Parents help children have equilibrium at all ages by providing not just bonding and love, but by being engaged, safe, and predictable.

*1. In what ways are you closely involved in your toddler's or preschooler's life? What could you be doing to show your child that you are interested in his life?

2. Do you think your toddler finds you safe enough? Predictable enough? On what do you base your answer?

---

*This is the most important question, but try to spend a little time on all of the questions under your groups goal.

3. We build relationship by communicating our love. What way(s) of showing your love does your child respond to most enthusiastically?

Goal #2: Learn basic trust and need. Basic trust is your child's ability to see the world of relationships as having enough goodness for her. You can help foster basic trust by being a "good enough" parent; that is, being responsive at the right times and in the right ways without being perfect—just a lot more good than bad.

*1. Describe what a "good enough" parent would do in two or three frequent parenting situations you face (e.g., a three-year-old who is chattering nonstop; the day's third spilled glass of milk; failure to share a toy; grabbing something from another child; a preschooler interrupting rather than waiting a turn; a toddler who wants you to read the current favorite book for the fourth time in a row).

2. What are you modeling about having needs and getting them met in a healthy way?

Goal #3: Value relationships. One aspect of maturity is being able to value and appreciate other people's love and sacrifice for us. This creates in children important traits like a heart of gratitude for others and the ability to seek out and connect to people who treat them right.

*1. What are you (or could you be) doing to teach your toddler or preschooler that her actions affect you and sometimes even hurt you?

2. What are you doing to teach and require heartfelt gratitude?

3. What are you (or could you be) doing to teach your toddler or preschooler about interactive conversation, about both talking and listening?

Goal #4: Internalize love. An important milestone for your child is to be able to soothe himself when you are not there. Your child's many experiences of safety and consistency combine over time into a stable internal mental and emotional representation of you. Ultimately, a child doesn't think, "Mom loves me, so I'm okay," but, "I'm a loved person, and I'm okay."

*1. Going to sleep in their own beds, learning to feed themselves, and staying in the care of babysitters all help children become more independent. What steps like these are you regularly allowing your child to take? Give specific examples.

2. In what ways are you being there for your child—for the fun stuff (reading books and playing ball) as well as the necessary "life" stuff (feeding, bathing, clothing, etc.)—in quantity as well as quality? Be specific.

Goal #5: Develop capacity for loss. Success in life involves learning to deal with loss. An attached child learns to protest, mourn, and resolve loss by bringing loss to relationship and eventually letting go. Children who don't attach may devalue what they lose, stay stuck in a protest mode, or chronically mourn.

1. How does your child typically deal with loss?

*2. With what kinds of words do you sympathize with your child's loss (the fact that she's not getting what she wants when she wants it, for instance)? Note: Don't change your mind and alter the limits so that your child can avoid sadness! The lesson that action teaches isn't helpful!

3. What are you modeling about how to deal with loss?

Goal #6: Develop gender roles. As kids grow into the preschool years, they begin learning how to attach to same sex and different sex people in distinctive ways. Little boys want both to be like and to compete with Dad; little girls do the same with Mom. Girls want to marry their dad, and boys, their mom. Parents need to help their kids structure these intense feelings.

1. What evidence have you seen that your preschool child is wanting both to be like and to compete with the same-sex parent?

°2. What are you saying to contain and structure the expression of these feelings?

Goal #7: Relate to the world. Children use relationship as a spring-board of safety from which to explore the world of preschool, games, imagination, sports, and peers. Connectedness helps children sort through what they like and don't like.

1. What aspects of the world is your child currently exploring? What are you doing to encourage that exploration?

*2. What is your child liking and not liking these days? What are you doing to further develop her interests in sports, art, music, or a specific skill? What might you do to broaden her horizons?

Goal #8: Develop give-and-take. Another aspect of growing up is learning that relationships require give-and-take. The other person doesn't exist for the child and also has needs that have to be met in this relationship.

1. The ability to understand give-and-take develops during the early school years. What evidence do you see in your child that he isn't there yet, that he sees connections with people in terms of his own interests?

*2. What are you modeling about give-and-take in the relationships your child witnesses you in?

Goal #9: Teach altruism. The most mature attachment skill is self-less giving. Altruism is giving out of concern for another, without regard to oneself. It is the essence of God's love.

°1. What opportunities to begin to teach altruism to your toddler or preschooler do you find in your family? In play groups? In church settings?

2. What selfless love (not martyr love, but a love based on free and good-natured choice) are you showing to your child? Consider times you've expressed empathy or gratitude. When, if ever, have you been able to reward your child for showing compassion for friends?

How Attachment Happens

Specific tasks create the ability to _____. The child has his job, and the mother (or primary caregiver) has hers. These two jobs interact to help the child become capable of making attachments to people.

First, the child must experience the reality that

_____ is good and that it brings the necessary elements of life. His first task is to _____ and

_____ to the _____ for relationship. When he is lonely, afraid, anxious, hurt, or hungry, he needs to pay attention to his discomfort and respond to it in some way.

Closely related is the second task. The child must

_____ long enough for help to get to him. Love and support don't always come instantly.

Finally, a child's third task is to _____ the

_____. One of the main jobs of a child's first year is to take in love through thousands of loving experiences.

What is the parent's task? Simply put, a parent needs to

_____ to the child's needs with _____,

_____, and _____. A parent must also respond _____. And, as the child gets older, a parent must _____ without being

_____.

Parent your child to be able safely to _____ and

_____ love and connectedness. You are helping build a connected foundation inside her that will sustain her for life.

DEVELOPING SELF-CONTROL: RESPONSIBILITY

- The task of parenting is to transform the child's stance from "My life is my parents' problem" to "Yikes, my life is my problem! My parents love me, but they aren't going to clean up all the messes I make in life."
- We define responsibility as the capacity to own one's life as one's problem. It is the parents' job to help structure their children's time and energy into activities that develop responsibility.
- Choices between good and bad and information about the dangers of the bad are definitely important to a child's decision-making. But children also need to be given the opportunity to learn responsibility by doing—by practicing self-control, delaying gratification, and setting and receiving limits.
- From the beginning, the child has no interest whatsoever in becoming responsible. But taking on responsibilities for your children that they should be bearing themselves negates and stifles their ability to shoulder life as they grow up.
- Setting boundaries is a central part of developing responsible character in your child. Boundaries are a person's property line. They allow you to know what you are and are not responsible for. And wise parents appropriately structure their children's lives so that their children are free to make choices that will either reward them for responsibility or cause them pain for irresponsibility.
- The fruits of responsibility in a child's life are ownership, self-control, and freedom from bondage to childlike things like his impulses, intense emotions, peer pressure, and pleasure-based thinking. A free child has learned the blessings of owning and choosing well—and that's definitely character!

SETTING CONSEQUENCES AND SHOWING LOVE

Review the following list of qualities that make consequences effective. Give a real-life example or two of when consequences were (or could have been) ...

—As close to natural consequences as possible

—Appropriate to the child's developmental maturity level

—Appropriately severe

—Administered ASAP

—Loving

—As specific as possible

SUGGESTED READING

"Laying the Foundation of Life: Connectedness" and "Developing Self-Control: Responsibility," chapters 4 and 5 of *Raising Great Kids*

TAKING IT HOME

CONNECTING

1. Look again at the nine attachment goals you considered in the "What's a Parent to Do?" exercise. Finish working through the questions. Then choose one goal to work on this week and take a specific step toward that goal.

2. Whether your child needs connection for her isolation, hurt, or loneliness or needs answers, suggestions, advice, and problem solving for her functional needs, what do you do (or could you do) to teach her that relationship comes before anything? By what words and actions do you try to show understanding, warmth, and empathy? How do you show your child that you are listening to her? How, for instance, do you help draw out her feelings so that she learns that feelings are okay? In what ways do you or could you stay connected to her when she protests? What do you do to make sure you understand your child's emotions before you address or try to contain them?

3. Sticking a bottle in a lonely infant's mouth is an example of an attempt to solve a relational problem functionally. Evaluate your tendency to solve relational problems functionally. Is it a problem? If so, under what circumstances are you most likely to do so?

4. Often we can think we're communicating love to someone, adult or child. But what we're doing or saying may not feel like love to the recipient. What words or actions most clearly communicate love to your child? If you're not sure, become a student of your child. Do gifts, time, hugs, words, notes, or something else seem to make your child feel most loved? If you know what makes your child feel loved, consider how often you speak that language of love to him or her—and start making it a habit if it isn't already.

RESPONSIBILITY

1. What boundaries have you set—or could you set—for your children that reward them for responsibility? First think of a responsibility your young child is capable of assuming. What boundaries have you set—or could you set—for your children that cause them pain for irresponsibility? Again, first think of a responsibility your young child is capable of assuming. For example, could you enforce a clean-up routine with the consequence of losing a toy for a certain length of time?

2. In what small ways can you give your toddler or preschooler some practice in self-control? Delaying gratification? Honoring limits you set? Could you, for instance, set limits and establish consequences for tantrums rather than nagging, pleading, or threatening?

3. The next time you need to reinforce the importance of following rules or truth, a tangible fence or boundary might help. Take your child to a local fenced-in playground, ideally next to a busy street. Talk about how easy and safe it would be to play ball since the fence surrounds the play area. Then get your child thinking about what it would be like to try to play on the playground if the fence were gone. Help your child conclude that fences (boundaries) mean safety and protection. Explain as simply as possible that your rules do the same job that fence does: give your child safety and protection.

Pray for your kids!

—Session Four—
Developing Reality and Competence

OVERVIEW

✦ Losing well is one of the most important character traits parents can develop in their children.

✦ Kids need help dealing with imperfection in themselves, in other people, and in the world.

✦ For a child, being loved should become more central than being good enough.

✦ Developing competence and skill in certain areas helps children take their place in, and contribute to, the adult world.

✦ Parents need to show their kids that work is good, important, and expected.

✦ Parents need to help kids develop competency areas as well as learn the disciplines of work.

Living in an Imperfect World: Reality

- Losing well, with the ability to continue on, is one of the most important character traits you can develop in your child. We need to teach children to lose because they live in reality, and reality is a place where things do not always go as we would like.

- Learning to accept both the good and the bad enables children to have a firm grounding in reality and to create a life that will help them pursue what's left of Eden, without giving up along the way.

- In this world of tribulation, children are going to have to learn to overcome imperfection in three spheres: self, other people, and the world.

- Children need to learn to accept their own imperfection and to live with imperfection in others. They need to develop the character that will enable them to be joyful in a world that daily gives them opportunity to be miserable. Children need the character to overcome losses, failure, sin, and evil—in themselves, in others, and in the world around them.

- When something goes wrong in life, we tend to make sure that neither we nor anyone else knows the truth. Our attempts to hide the fact that something has gone wrong are aptly symbolized by Adam and Eve's fig leaves. Four such strategies—barriers to building the character your child needs—are denial of the bad things, denial of the ideals, judgment of the bad, and lack of experience of the bad things in life.

- These barriers keep children from (1) learning from their mistakes, (2) realizing they're not as good as they think they are, (3) realizing that failure doesn't cost them love, (4) acknowledging that they do not know everything or know how to do everything, and (5) becoming whole by integrating the "good me–bad me" split inside them. Clearly, we parents need to let our kids face reality.

The idea of self-esteem is confusing for several reasons. First, the idea of self-esteem places the _____ of children at risk by basing it on their positive _____. Second, the focus is on maintaining a good view of ourselves as opposed to maintaining _____. Third, the "good self" is a proud self, and a proud self does not develop the kind of _____ before God and others that results in _____.

In making these points against positive self-esteem, Drs. Cloud and Townsend are not saying that children should not be praised for doing well. Children were created with a need for parental _____, so praise them for a job well done. Validating their ability to do something consolidates a feeling of _____ in children and helps them _____ that feeling.

Neither are the doctors advocating the viewpoint that we are only dirty rotten sinners. We are both bearers of God's image and sinners. The real question is where the safety comes from that allows us to be all that we are. And the Bible's answer to that is love (1 John 4:18).

So the doctors say, "Don't buy into the philosophy that building positive self-esteem is the answer to all of the child's problems." Children need, most of all, to feel _____ as they are and then to be _____ to learn how to do things well. The issue of "Am I good enough?" will become a nonissue. A "_____ self" is much more secure than a "_____ self" any day.

Furthermore, making children feel bad does not motivate them to do better. Nor does making them feel good guard them from all of life's pitfalls. The answer to the self-esteem problem is this: Give them

a combination of _____ and _____,
and they will feel _____ enough to be _____.

Children need to learn what (hopefully) their parents have already learned: they need to know that it is okay to _____, to _____, or to be less than _____. They need to feel secure in bringing their _____ parts to relationship.

There is no problem that the _____ and guidance of _____ parents cannot get children through. But if children do not feel they can be who they really are, then their problems never get solved. They just get hidden away to grow into bigger cancers.

THE FIVE-STEP PROCESS OF EMBRACING REALITY

1. *Protest.* Give an example of a time when reality hit your child. In what ways did she (quite naturally) protest that reality, be it the pain of separation, discipline, or something else?

2. *Reality remains.* When have you let the reality of discipline stand rather than relenting after your child's protest? What do parents teach their children if they rush in to change painful realities?

3. *Metabolize the reality.* What empathy (which is grace communicated and a means by which your child experiences your love) did you extend your child in the example you just gave? How did your child respond to that empathy?

4. *Grief.* Consider again your child's response to the empathy you offered. What evidence of mourning and then of letting go did you see? Be specific.

5. *Problem solving and resolution.* Still working with your example, what did you do to help your child learn why she failed and to encourage her to try again? If the example was in the area of performance, did your child "get back on the horse"? If the example was in the area of relationship, did your child confront, repent, forgive, and reconcile?

VIDEO SEGMENT

DEVELOPING GIFTS AND TALENTS: COMPETENCE

- The adult club has requirements for membership. The first requirement is to be competent in some area. The second is to become equal and mutual with adults (competent people show themselves to be brothers and sisters to other adults, with God as their parent). The third requirement for adulthood is relational. Adults connect on both a bonding and a task level. Developing some skill or expertise helps your child relate in both ways to other adults.

- The ability of children to master some gift or talent is an important source of a realistic self-image and confidence.

- Children should *not* have their love needs tied to their performance. Throughout their children's lives, parents need to clearly communicate, "I love you with no strings attached. However, I don't approve of how you are handling the jobs we are giving you."

- Children need to hear that work is good, important, and expected. In fact, helping children develop competency first involves helping them develop a "pro-work" attitude.

- Children need to make friends with work early in life and understand that it is just as much a part of life as attachment, friends, and fun. A parent's job is to help structure, focus, and deepen children's involvement in their work.

Making It Happen

Work and Skill Are Part of Life

Directions

Below you'll find a comprehensive tool to help you evaluate what you are modeling about interest in, involvement in, and even frustration with work you do inside as well as outside the home. Take five minutes on your own to read through the questions. You'll have more time to work on this exercise at home this week.

1. Values

Your work is, at some level, tied into your values. Think about the tasks you do within the home as well as the kind of work you do outside the home, if any. What does your young child understand about why you do what you do and why you think it's important?

2. Habits

Model your work ethics and habits and let your child start developing her own work habits. What household task do you (or could you) let your child do with minimum parental supervision? (Picking up the play area, getting the cereal box off the shelf at the grocery store, and getting pajamas and perhaps even putting them on are a few possibilities.) As your child gets older, what consequences might be appropriate for work not completed without supervision?

3. Attitudes

Grumbling has been a part of work life ever since the Fall. You can't ask children to whistle while they work, but you can require them to keep their protests respectful. What are you doing to show your children that you appreciate their beginning efforts to work around the house (picking up their toys, helping to set the table, sweeping the front walkway, etc.)?

4. Normalization

Normalize work both inside and outside the home for your children. Let them know that you expect them to work most of their life. What work around the house can help your young child learn that work is a normal and ongoing aspect of life?

5. Delegation

Children should be shouldering age-appropriate tasks. What tasks are age-appropriate for your child—and what kind of enthusiastic commentary about those tasks will help your child realize that the family is a team and the team works together?

6. Work and Money

We don't believe in paying a child for chores. We suggest instead that, on a regular basis, you give your children some money not tied to chores. This can generally begin around kindergarten age when your child is learning about numbers and money issues.

Although your child is too young to be tithing, saving, and spending, take a few moments now to consider how and when you might want to implement such a program.

7. Skill

In work, it's not enough to show up and participate. Results do matter. Help your child learn the importance of skill and achievement. What problems can result from parents demanding too much? From parents being afraid to challenge their child? What can you do to be sure you're not asking either too little or too much of your child?

8. Creativity and Problem-Solving

The heart of work is creating good things and solving problems. Getting children involved in tasks is inviting them to discover these fundamental aspects of work. What can you do (or not do!) so that your child finds herself in the role of problem-solver as she tackles an age-appropriate task? In what situation, for instance, can you empathize with the difficulty of the problem, but not rescue her and keep her from learning by doing the task at hand? What benefit comes to your child when you empathize rather than do the task for her?

9. Evaluation

It helps kids to be graded on their performance. They need to experience success and failure. Being graded helps them monitor their ways and make necessary corrections. It reinforces responsibility and punishes slothfulness. Why isn't it helpful to eliminate failure from a child's experience? What does it mean to you to "fail well"— and what will you do to teach your child to fail well?

10. Competition

Mastering tasks often involves some conflict with and comparison to other children. Help your child know how to compete well. However, competition should not be a big deal in the early years. What does "competing well" mean to you? As they grow older, what will you do to teach your children how to compete well and how to accept loss?

11. Fears of Success and Failure

Children will most likely struggle with fears of both doing well and failing in life. These two different struggles have much to do with their relationship with you as the parent. How can your unconditional love for your children help keep these fears from taking root and later even incapacitating them?

MAKING IT HAPPEN

DEVELOPING TALENTS AND GIFTS

Directions

Please take 5 minutes to start working on this exercise. Once again, you'll finish this exercise at home this week.

1. *Discovering Talents.* Within the souls of children are certain aptitudes waiting to emerge and bloom into talents and gifts. God has done his job, and your job is to invite your children to engage in various experiences so that you and they can figure out what they value, excel in, and love doing.

> What do you want to do and not do to help your children find out what they love and excel in? And what might you do to make your children's environment stimulus-rich? What interactive toys and art supplies encourage them to imagine and create?

2. *Development.* Invite your children to discover their interests. And when they have latched onto some interest and invested time and energy in it, challenge them to develop their talent. Preschoolers don't keep their (sometimes rather short-lived) interests a secret.

> What is your preschooler interested in, or what has she been interested in? What kind of encouragement to pursue those interests did she or is she receiving?

3. *The Basics.* All the while that you are guiding your children toward mastery in specialty areas, they should also be gaining competency in the universal areas of life that all adults need—areas such as academics, problem solving, social skills, language, hygiene and health, and home maintenance.

> Your preschooler has not yet entered the world of academics, but what are you doing—and could you be doing—to help him gain competence in the following areas? Be specific. It's not too early to start healthy lifelong habits.
>
> Problem solving
>
>
> Social skills
>
>
> Language
>
>
> Hygiene and health
>
>
> Home maintenance

4. *The Parent as Background.* Understand your role in helping children develop mastery. You are in the background, providing a structure for them to experience growth. Don't get caught feeling that your success is measured by your children's success. And don't become overinvolved in your child's activities because of your own needs. Don't control the rate of accomplishment; let the experts guide. Don't center your child's life around her gift. And don't idealize your child.

> To which of the dangers just listed might you be most vulnerable as you parent your child? Think now about how to prevent that behavior.

"Living in an Imperfect World: Reality" and "Developing Gifts and Talents: Competence," chapters 6 and 7 of *Raising Great Kids*

Taking It Home

Reality

In this world of tribulation, we all have to learn to overcome imperfection in three spheres: self, other people, and the world.

1. **Self.** What are you doing to teach your children that it is okay to fail and to be less than perfect? Think about the behaviors they see in you as well as the words they hear from you as you react to your failures and imperfections. Also, how do you help your children face and accept the reality that they are flawed, imperfect people who will fail, lose, and make mistakes?

2. **Other People.** We also need to learn that other people are not perfect. We want others to gratify us, to never make mistakes, and certainly to never hurt us. What have you said—and what would you like to say—to your children about the fact that other people are not perfect?

3. **The World.** Not only will we frustrate ourselves and be frustrated by others, but the world will frustrate us as well. Think about a time the world frustrated your child. Perhaps a pet died or a birthday party was rained out or a toy broken. What did you do or say to help your child cope with that loss? What are you doing to teach your children that it is okay to hurt? What do they see about how you deal with hurt? What do they receive and hear from you when they are hurt?

2. COMPETENCE

During the session, you read through two exercises, "Work and Skill Are Part of Life" and "Developing Talents and Gifts." Complete these exercises and then choose one point from each to put into practice this week.

If you don't have time to do any or all of the above, do make time to pray! Ask the Lord to continue to be at work building character in your child.

—Session Five—
Developing Morality and Spirituality

OVERVIEW

✦ A child's sense of moral awareness involves several elements which together form a mature conscience.

✦ The purpose of the conscience is both to protect love and to align itself with God's reality.

✦ Children develop conscience through identification, imitation, modeling, and experience.

✦ A child's spiritual life needs to be centered on connecting to God as the Author of reality.

✦ Parents need to present to their children spiritual life integrated with everyday life.

✦ Parents need to teach kids the spiritual disciplines and give them experiences to internalize them.

MAKING A CONSCIENCE: MORALITY

- God has granted parents the responsibility for developing their child's sense of moral awareness.
- This moral awareness includes the following:

    - An awareness of right and wrong;
    - The morals that will guide your child;
    - An internal ability to weigh moral decisions;
    - An ability to self-correct;
    - A proper internal response to violating a standard; and
    - A desire to do right.

- Parents worry. Three things worth worrying about are:

    1. That your children develop a conscience (both a moral awareness of right or wrong and the inclination to follow in the right direction and enforce internal consequences if they do wrong).
    2. The tone of the conscience (e.g., if the tone of the child's conscience is angry, guilt-producing, and condemning, that conscience becomes the adversary).
    3. The content and quality of the conscience (the content will change as your child grows, but the focus should be relationship, reality issues, reality consequences, protecting love with God and others, and aligning oneself with the reality of God's created order rather than petty rules).

- Your laws become part of your children's consciences through identification, imitation, modeling, and experience.
- If the two parents are not on the same page, a child may end up with a "split conscience." In other words, a child's conscience may end up with a strict part and a permissive part. Continuously compare with your spouse how the two of you are doing in balancing the tone, content, and quality of being the external conscience for your children.

YOUR FAMILY'S TEN COMMANDMENTS

One _____ is enough for anyone to deal with. We want our child's conscience to be a _____, not an _____. We want the focus of that conscience to be _____, _____ issues, and _____ consequences. We want the conscience to work toward protecting _____ with God and others and toward aligning oneself with the reality of God's created _____ more than with petty rules.

Unfortunately, petty rules and even very unhealthy rules contribute to the formation of the conscience. As Dr. Cloud said, "Just as God gave his family (the children of Israel) a set of commandments to follow, parents give their family their own set. It is given not in stone, but with _____."

Think about the set of commandments your parents gave you as you were growing up. Some possibilities are "Thou shalt not speak the truth about certain issues. It will make your father angry"; "Thou shalt not make a mistake ever. You should already know how to do it before you are told"; and "Thou shalt not be independent. It is an abomination."

No family would put such commandments on the wall of the kitchen in embroidery to be memorized. But commandments like these are _____ because they are _____ by the children and become part of their own conscience. Later in life, when a relationship calls for direct truth or independence, the child's conscience will not allow him to bring forth those qualities. As a result, his adult relationships suffer. Remember, no matter what you believe, how you _____ to your children is forming their conscience. Their brains are recording your _____ to them.

Directions

1. On your own, please take a few minutes to reflect on the good values listed below.
2. Choose three values and answer the questions listed on page 67.
3. You will have 10 minutes to complete this exercise.

GOOD VALUES

- Love, honor, obedience, and the pursuit of God (seek him first in everything)
- Love and its derivatives: compassion, forgiveness, mercy, grace, kindness
- Truth and its derivatives: honesty, integrity, directness, taking moral stands, confession, respect for reality
- Humility
- Faith (acting and ordering life on things unseen)
- Faithfulness and loyalty
- Service and sacrifice (giving, offering, and sacrificing of self for others and higher values)
- Stewardship (taking God's gifts and one's possessions seriously)
- Respect (for other people and their property)
- Obedience and submission (to God, parents, law and government, and other legitimate authority)
- Self-control and self-discipline (delay of gratification)
- Courage (faith, risk-taking, and pushing on through fear)
- Sexual wholeness (purity, respect for God's creation, limits, embracing and celebrating sexuality)
- Fun (celebration and enjoyment of life and God's blessings and creation)
- Development of talents and work (congruence with pursuing the true self that God created)
- Furthering God's life to others (evangelism, missions, helping)

1. What are you teaching your children about each of these three values through your words—and what do you want to be teaching them? What further steps will you take to teach those lessons?

2. What are you teaching your children about each of these three values by your actions—and what do you want to be teaching them? What additional steps will you take to teach those lessons?

CONNECTING TO GOD: WORSHIP AND SPIRITUAL LIFE

- To grow up, children need to order their lives around the Author of reality. Finding and responding to God's statutes and ways becomes the key to growing up.
- Our spiritual life is meant to be integrated into all aspects of our relationships and tasks. Spiritual character growth, therefore, involves much more than religious training; it involves helping the child experience that the essence of existence is spiritual.
- Spiritual life begins with a relationship between your child and God. But a relationship requires two willing parties. You can't force your child to develop a relationship with God. God invites, but does not force himself on you or your child.
- A parent's task is to create a structure or develop a context that fosters connectedness to God. To create optimal conditions for your child to meet and love God:

    —Help your child see the eternal in the everyday: Your child needs to experience how you interpret circumstances from a transcendent viewpoint.
    —Help your child see God as the Source of all good things. As one parent put it, "We are working on helping our son learn that God is a better parent to him than we are."
    —Help your child see that life works better living it God's way. Teach how God's "house rules" of love, fairness, faithfulness, and honesty make all of life work well in the same way that traffic lights and stop signs make our driving better and safer.
    —Help your child internalize the disciplines of spiritual life— prayer and fellowship, as well as the study of, memorization of, and meditation on God's Word.

- You are helping your child make a shift from immature to mature dependency on God the Father.

MAKING IT HAPPEN

YOUR FAITH MATTERS TO YOUR CHILD'S FAITH

Directions

On your own, take five minutes to read through and begin thinking about the issues raised in the questions below.

1. What stories of your own doubts, struggles with God, and failings to be the person he wants you to be will you regularly share with your children as they grow up? How will you let them see that a relationship with God, like a relationship with anyone, takes time, has conflict, and requires work?

2. Your children were created to seek and find God. What opportunities to draw close to God are you giving your child? What experiences (for example, being around good people who love our good God) do you want to be sure to provide your children as they grow up?

THE AGE OF FAITH

Directions

Please divide into groups of three or four. You will have 10 minutes to discuss with your group the questions you see listed.

What one or two activities can you do with your children to help them begin to understand the following basic gospel truths so that they can make an authentic decision for Christ?

- The existence and love of God (as we've said, point out his involvement in your everyday life)

- The reality of our sinful state (preschoolers can understand the struggle of wanting to do the right thing but being unable to do so)

- The penalty of sin and God's provision through the death of Christ (Easter is a great opportunity for this)

- The requirement of accepting Christ personally (talk about the difference between knowing *about* God and knowing God)

THE GIFT—AND THE POWER—OF PRAYER

Directions

1. Divide into groups of three or four.
2. Using the list below, take turns praying for your children to develop the six character traits we have talked about during the past few weeks. Also pray for each of them to one day make a decision for Christ.
3. You'll have 8 minutes to pray with your group.

Six Traits Every Child Needs

- Connectedness
- Responsibility
- Reality
- Competence
- Morality
- Worship and spiritual life

Suggested Reading

"Making a Conscience: Morality" and "Connecting to God: Worship and Spiritual Life," chapters 8 and 9 of *Raising Great Kids*

Taking It Home

1. Review the values listed on page 66. What are you teaching your children about each of these values by your actions? By your words? What do you want to be teaching your kids about these good values? What will you do to teach those lessons?

2. What fellow believer can help you see what kind of faith you model to people around you? Talk to that person about your strengths as well as your weaknesses and ask for prayer as you seek to lead a life of faith that you want your children to "catch" and follow.

3. Spend some more time thinking about the questions raised in "Your Faith Matters to Your Child's Faith."

4. Starting now, be a student of your children. Get to know each one's character (is he private or outgoing; does she want to figure things out for herself or is she always teachable; etc.) so that you will have a better idea of your role in inviting them to name Jesus as their Savior and Lord.

5. Praying is the most important step you can take toward becoming the parent you want to be! Take time to pray for your children and your parenting every day this week.

—Session Six—
When in Doubt, Connect!

OVERVIEW

✤ Temperament is an inborn style of relating to the world, and that style is different in different children.

✤ Character is the ability to function in life. It is more important than temperament.

✤ Temperament should not excuse improper behavior; it can be modified with experience.

✤ Your child is also God's child—and he will not forsake his own.

✤ Parenting cannot be done in a vacuum—you need supportive relationships.

✤ When you don't know how to deal with a problem with your child, your first move is to connect with him or her.

UNDERSTANDING TEMPERAMENTS

- Temperament is not the same as character. Temperament is a style of relating to the world. It is inborn. Character, however, is a set of necessary abilities to function in the world, and each of us is responsible for developing all the character traits in ourselves.
- Character development should make allowances for differences in temperament, but character and temperament are not equal. Character comes first; style, or temperament, second.
- It's sometimes difficult to tell if a problem is temperament- or character-based. But when character issues are resolved, the remaining temperament issues don't tend to be a major problem.
- If you see a behavioral tendency you are concerned about, investigate it first as a character issue. Most of the time the answer lies in character.
- Imagine children who are struggling with an issue that is 0 percent character and 100 percent temperament. If that's the case, even though their temperament is not their fault, they are increasingly responsible for dealing with it as they grow up. Furthermore, they need to make temperament change a matter of growing in character.
- Deal with temperament when it inhibits growth in connectedness, responsibility, reality, competence, morality, and spiritual life.
- Temperaments can be modified with experience. This is a testimony to the redemptive work of God: Our traits don't determine our lives.

CHARACTER OR TEMPERAMENT?

If you see a tendency you are concerned about, a good rule of thumb is to investigate it first as a character issue. For example, if your child intrudes on others, interrupts, and is pushy, this problem could be driven by a lack of self-control (a character issue), or by an energetic temperament. Ask yourself the following questions:

Is she seeking _____ the only way she
  knows how?

Is she unaware of how her _____ affects
  others?

Is she _____ people?

Is she operating without any _____?

Does she provoke others as a way to make them set
  _____ with her?

Does the behavior show a lack of personal _____
  and _____?

Is your child trying to cover up _____ and
  _____ by being aggressive?

Could your child's behavior be a response to her inner
  _____?

These questions need to be fine-tuned to match the specific behavior problem you're dealing with, but they give you a model for how to determine whether the problem is one of temperament or character. Most of the time the answer lies in character. When _____ issues are resolved, the remaining _____ issues don't tend to be a major problem.

A CHILD I LOVE

Directions

1. On your own, spend a minute or two assessing your child's temperament. To get you started, choose from among the traits you see listed below and then add a few more ideas of your own to paint as complete a picture of your child as possible.
2. With the time remaining, reflect on and answer the questions in light of your assessment.
3. You will have 10 minutes to complete this exercise.

Traits			
Easygoing	Funny	Intuitive	
Active	Willing to take risks	Quiet	
Inwardly-directed	Creative		
Sociable	Logical		

1. Where, if at all, is your child's temperament inhibiting growth in any of the six areas of character growth (connectedness, responsibility, reality, competence, morality, worship and spiritual life) we've been considering? Your toddler, for example, may by nature be more energetic than other children. If this is the case, he may need you to help him learn self-control by giving him a strong but loving set of boundaries and consequences.

2. How will relationship with you help your child deal with the aspect(s) of character growth you addressed in the preceding question?

THE DIVINE VIEW

- Understand your parenting from God's point of view. God chose you to be your child's parent. Remember that the Lord is helping, guiding, and supporting you, and he is not surprised by the twists and turns of the process. The parenting job is a large one, but not too large for you and God. He trusts you with the child he has given you, and he has equipped you for the task. Remember, too, that your child is also God's child, and he will not forsake his own (Deuteronomy 31:6).

- Parents need support. The Lord will indeed support your parenting efforts, but you also need the help and support of others. After all, you don't have everything your child needs, and you need to get what you don't possess from warm, honest people. You need to be in regular, vulnerable contact with people who are helping you grow not only as a parent but also to grow personally and spiritually as an individual.

- Use this book as a road map pointing you to the six areas in which your child needs to be growing. So familiarize yourself with the six character traits and address them.

- Normalize failure. The sad reality is that you have failed in the past and you will fail in the future. Be a parent who is not afraid of failure, but sees it as a way to grow. Be less afraid of mistakes and more afraid of denying them.

- When in doubt, connect. Connection never hurts, often helps, and sometimes is the entire solution to the problem. Teach your child by word and deed that being in relationship is very important. And may you know God's blessing as you continue to seek what is best for your child.

1. Why is relationship the most important of all the character aspects discussed in this book?

2. When you encounter an unsolvable problem, take steps to move toward your children in a way that they can experience that you are with and for them and that you want to understand their internal world. What kinds of steps could you take that would be appropriate and meaningful for your preschooler?

BEING PARENTS WHO PRAY

Directions

1. Break into groups of four or five.
2. Using the suggestions below as a guideline for your group prayer. You will have 8 minutes to pray for your children.

Give thanks for . . .

Your children
God's sovereignty
God's availability to you as you parent

Confess . . .

Sins that interfere with your parenting
Discouragement
Fear

Request . . .

The Lord to help you parent with grace *and* truth
God to bless the time you spend with your kids
Wisdom, hope
Support in your parenting efforts
Creativity
Patience, love
God to work in the heart of your child(ren)
Your children come to name Jesus as Lord and Savior

Lay before the Lord any current parenting issues, challenges, or problems.

Suggested Reading

"Understanding Temperaments" and "When in Doubt, Connect!" chapter 12 and the conclusion in *Raising Great Kids*

Taking It Home

- Choose three or four verses from Scripture that are especially encouraging to you as a parent. Memorize them so that they are hidden in your heart that you might not sin against your child or the Lord. Let them be a source of encouragement when the demands of parenting temporarily outweigh the joys.
- Keep praying! Find encouragement in the following truths that are well worth repeating:

    God chose you to be your child's parent.

    The Lord is helping, guiding, and supporting you, and he is not surprised by the twists and turns of the process.

    The parenting job is a large one, but not too large for you and God.

    He trusts you with the child he has given you, and he has equipped you for the task.

A Special Letter to Mothers of Preschoolers

You have just completed a curriculum about parenting your young child. No doubt you have found encouragement and instruction that will help you in the task of parenting.

Would you like ongoing encouragement and support? That's what MOPS is all about.

MOPS stands for Mothers of Preschoolers, a program designed for mothers with children under school age. Women in MOPS come from different backgrounds and lifestyles, yet have similar needs and a shared desire to be the best mothers they can be!

A MOPS group provides a caring, accepting atmosphere for all mothers of preschoolers. Here you have the opportunity to share concerns, explore areas of creativity and hear instruction that will continue to equip you for the responsibilities of family and community. The MOPS program also includes MOPPETS, a loving, learning experience for children. Approximately 2,500 MOPS groups currently meet in churches in the United States and 11 other countries, to meet the needs of more than 100,000 women.

MOPS also offers:

- Leadership training through resources, workshops, and mentoring. The MOPS group is primarily led by the mothers themselves, with the assistance of a MOPS Mentor.
- Connection to an international network of leaders through newsletters, a radio program, conventions, and a web site.
- A dynamic, time-tested program that has proven effective in many adaptations, including suburban, urban, teen, rural, and international settings. When you start a MOPS group, you will receive all the materials you need to begin a successful MOPS program.

- The MOPS Shop featuring books and quality products specifically designed for mothers of preschoolers.
- An outreach ministry, through the local church, to mothers of preschoolers. Specially designed resources, available through MOPS, train moms in lifestyle evangelism.

To receive information such as how to join a MOPS group, or how to receive other MOPS resources such as Mom Sense newsletter, call or write MOPS International, P.O. Box 102200, Denver, CO 80250-2200. Phone 1-800-929-1287. E-mail: Info@MOPS.org. Web site: http://www.MOPS.org. To learn how to start a MOPS group, call 1-888-910-MOPS.

EMBARK ON A
LIFE-CHANGING JOURNEY
OF PERSONAL AND SPIRITUAL GROWTH

DR. HENRY CLOUD   **DR. JOHN TOWNSEND**

Dr. Henry Cloud and Dr. John Townsend have been bringing hope and healing to millions for over two decades. They have helped people everywhere discover solutions to life's most difficult personal and relational challenges. Their material provides solid, practical answers and offers guidance in the areas of *parenting, singles issues, personal growth,* and *leadership.*

Bring either Dr. Cloud or Dr. Townsend to your church or organization. They are available for:

- Seminars on a wide variety of topics
- Training for small group leaders
- Conferences
- Educational events
- Consulting with your organization

Other opportunities to experience Dr. Cloud and Dr. Townsend:

- Ultimate Leadership workshops—held in Southern California throughout the year
- Small group curriculum
- Seminars via Satellite
- Solutions Audio Club—Solutions is a weekly recorded presentation

For other resources, and for dates of seminars and workshops
by Dr. Cloud and Dr. Townsend, visit:
www.cloudtownsend.com

For other information **Call (800) 676-HOPE (4673)**

Or write to:
Cloud-Townsend Resources
3176 Pullman Street, Suite 105
Costa Mesa, CA

We want to hear from you. Please send your comments about this book to us in care of zreview@zondervan.com. Thank you.

GRAND RAPIDS, MICHIGAN 49530 USA